STAY
FOCUSED

Jackie Flemming

STAY FOCUSED

Jackie Flemming

T&J Publishers
A Small Independent Publisher
with a Big Voice

Printed in the United States of America by T&J Publishers (Atlanta, GA.) www.TandJPublishers.com

All Bible verses used are from the King James Version (KJV), and the New Living Translation (NLT), and the New American Standard Bible (NASB), and the New International Version (NIV).

Cover design by Timothy Flemming, Jr.
Book format and layout by Timothy Flemming, Jr.

ISBN: 978-0-9962165-9-3

For more information, go to:
www.LadyJackie.com
Facebook: Jackie Flemming
Instagram: JackieFlemming1
Periscope: Jackie Flemming
Email: JackieFlemming1@gmail.com

Other books by Jackie Flemming:
Purpose Seekers (2014)
Purpose Seekers Journal (2014)
You Matter (2015)

Dedication

I dedicate this book first and foremost to my Lord and Savior, Jesus the Christ. Jesus, you mean everything to me. Without You, I don't know where I'd be today. Thank you for Your constant love and enduring grace.

To my husband, best friend, life's partner, publisher, producer, etc.: Timothy. I love you so much. You are amazing, and I thank God for you being in my life. God knows what He's doing when He joins two people together.

To my children: Timothy 3rd, Timera, and Jeremiah. I love you all so much. It is such a joy watching you all grow-up. You bring so much happiness to my life, and I know that God has awesome things in store for each of you.

To my parents (Shirley and Anthony), I love you both. Thank you for all that you have invested into me. Also, to all of my other family members, I love you all.

To my supporters, thank you for your prayers, words of encouragement, support, and all that you do. I can't thank you enough.

"One reason so few of us achieve what we truly want is that we never direct our focus; we never concentrate our power. Most people dabble their way through life, never deciding to master anything in particular."
—Toney Robbins

TABLE OF CONTENTS

INTRODUCTION
THE LAW
OF FOCUS

There is a very popular saying: Never start something that you can't finish. If you're going to start something, be prepared to finish it; be prepared to go all of the way. Setting out to accomplish goals entails being prepared to make sacrifices and doing whatever it takes to accomplish those goals. There is an art to accomplishing goals, but this art is one that isn't really taught in business schools; it is a skill that we primarily learn through trial and error and mistakes in our lives: it's the ability to focus and stay focused on our goals. And sadly, remaining focused in life is easier said than done. In fact, learning the art of focusing and staying focused is something people in the business world pay top dollar to learn in seminars and conferences. This art form is worth millions in and of itself. Why? Because once it's mastered by the individual, it will always lead to success, no matter what field a person is in. The art of focusing and staying focused works in every arena, from business to politics, from corporate America to ministry, academia and more. Even criminals use the techniques we are about to discuss in order to accomplish their illegal goals.

The biggest mistake made by many leaders, whether they be parents, school teachers, pastors, team/group leaders, supervisors, managers, etc. is to simply tell others to "stay focused" while forgetting that focusing is an actual skill that must be learned. In essence, there needs to be an actual class in school on how to study; there needs to be a training or peptalk on the job on how to focus and execute a task; there has to be a training in your church on how to study the Bible, and also a strong emphasis not just on what a new Believer should be focusing on, but to stay focused in a world of spiritual deception and distractions. Engaged couples need to be taught how to focus on each other, make time for one another, and keep the fire burning in their marriage during premarital counseling. The "how" entails laying out specific strategies and individual steps. Each of these steps and strategies is summed up in what I call The Law of Focus. (A law is "a system of rules enforced by a governing body.")

There is a system of rules and principles that has been passed down to us from God Himself, but it's been re-worded, repackaged, and represented by others as some "new truth" or "secret". But these laws are as old as Methuselah (in other words, they're divine laws dating back to the beginning of creation itself). Much like the law of gravity, it doesn't matter if you believe in these laws and principles or not—they exist and they've been proven to work.

Let's suppose you don't believe in the law of gravity. My challenge to you would be to attempt to disprove it by jumping off of the top of a skyscraper without a parachute on. You'd certainly become a believer in the law of gravity on your way down. The sad part, however, is by the time you discover that gravity is real in that scenario, it would already be too late for you. You would have foolishly plunged to a certain death. Likewise, there are goals and dreams that God has placed on the inside of you, and if you waste time debating over whether or not you should believe in these proven principles which I'm about to share, you may run the risk of finding out that they're real . . . at the expense of sacrificing precious time, opportunity and energy. Don't engage in useless time-stalling and mistakes that could have easily been prevented, and don't allow apprehension, fear and skepticism to cause you to plunge off of the cliff of opportunity without a parachute on which will send you to an unnecessary and destructive end. Don't waste time trying to figure things out on your own, especially when the path to success has already been laid out for you by others before you.

It was Solomon in the Bible who wrote,

"Fools think their own way is right, but the wise listen to others." (Proverbs 12:15, New Living Translation)

Solomon explains to us that the path to successfully accomplishing our goals has already been laid by God and practiced by others; therefore, if you simply follow the example set before by others who've used these principles in their own lives and have gained results, then you will experience results too. All I am doing is providing you with the principles that others have used, which God gave to us. Apply them to your life and you'll reap the benefits of them; ignore these principles you won't reap the benefits of them. Plain and simple.

Before I move forward and dive into the rest of this book I must reiterate to you what I just stated a second ago; you must allow this to sink down into your conscious mind: God has established a divine law which I call The Law of Focus. This law consists of several key principles and steps which you must follow to the "T", even if you may not understand them entirely. You are not about to read a couple of motivational tips meant to inspire you and make you feel good; instead, you are about to discover divine laws set in motion by God Himself, laws which are proven to work and are very scientific in nature. And yes, you'll be inspired by these revelations also. Keep that in mind as you read.

A law doesn't need your strength to work, nor

does it need you to believe in it to exist. A law exists with or without your consent. There is nothing mystical or spooky about The Law of Focus; it's practical and easy to understand though it may cause for you to stretch your thinking a little. If you do feel like it may require that you stretch your thinking a little bit in order to apply these principles, then I don't want you to be nervous about doing so. The act of learning in and of itself requires stretching your mind. If you are opposed to growing both physically and mentally, progressing, and learning, then you don't want to be stretched, you don't want to be challenged; therefore, you don't want to accomplish goals and live the life of your dreams, all of which requires doing that which may at times be uncomfortable to you in one way or another. Get ready to challenge yourself and grow personally in ways you've never grown before. There is a reason why you need to learn how to focus and also stay focused: you have a God-given destiny that you must fulfill. You have a purpose for being here, and fulfilling that purpose is determined by your ability to apply the principles that we're getting ready to cover.

I hope you're ready to get started! Get ready because your life is about to change! Let's begin!

CHAPTER 1
FOLLOW YOUR INSTINCTS

A PREDATOR IS A CREATURE THAT IS SURE ABOUT one thing in life: It knows what it wants. A lion doesn't have any confusion concerning its identity. It doesn't get confused over whether or not it belongs in the herd with the sheep or it belongs in the pride with the other lions. Lions know where they belong and what they're supposed to do for one reason: they have natural instincts that cause them to be the way that they are.

What is an instinct? *Instinct* is defined as "an innate, typically fixed pattern of behavior in animals in response to certain stimuli." Did you hear that? A "fixed pattern of behavior", one that you don't have to force yourself to engage in because you do it automatically without ever having to think about it. We have instincts that we engage in every day without even thinking about them: breathing, fear, and anxiety, the fight-or-flight syndrome (for example, when we are confronted with danger, our bodies naturally tense up and prepare to either fight that danger or run from it in an attempt to escape it. We don't even have to think about what to do in the situation because our bodies make that decision), and also sexual activity (once we reach puberty, we don't have to convince ourselves that the opposite sex is attractive and desirable; we automatically become attracted to the opposite sex without even fully knowing why. It just happens because it's...instinctual. We'll start to experience feelings of arousal and other physiological symptoms once seeing an attractive person, even without knowing what's going on with our bodies).

Just like you and I have been gifted by God

with natural instincts which we have no control over (now, let me make this clear: just because something is an instinct in your life, that doesn't mean you are powerless against it. You can't help the fact that you must breathe, but you can decide to hold your breath; also, you can't help that you may feel attracted to someone, but you can decide whether or not to engage in sexual immorality with that person. An instinct is just a natural desire, but you still have power over your desires—the power of "choice" is within your possession), we've also been gifted with what I call "purpose instincts". There are things we're naturally inclined towards, things that make us unique by design. There are certain areas and fields that cause us to naturally light up because they appeal to the natural proclivities w i t h i n us. All of our senses light up. We  smell the scent of blood there, and we find ourselves unconsciously concentrating much more intensely in that place. We seem to come alive while there. We've found our niches ("a situation or activity for which a person or thing is best suited; he place where a plant or animal is usually or naturally found"). A fish can't thrive on land, and a lion can't thrive in the ocean. You're quite in the office, but you roar like a mighty lion on the street or in the studio booth. You can't hold a note while singing, but you're a beast when it comes to organizing or decorating. It's in your blood. It's your nature. There's a place in this world where that which is inside you will thrive. You're not meant to thrive everywhere.

Maybe you're naturally drawn to fashion, or you are naturally drawn to acting and theater, or perhaps you are naturally drawn to debates and is argumentative by nature—a skill that is necessary for the law field as a lawyer. You might be a football player now, but you've always been a fitness freak whose goal and desire has always been to whip others into shape—a passion possessed only by personal trainers and fitness coaches. Or maybe you have a naturally talent for selling things; you're a natural salesman, a talent that not everyone has. You know how to convince people of things, focus on the needs of others and to execute the sale, whereas other people struggle with being able to mentally handle the challenges of overcoming rejection and not taking "no" for an answer, and also persistently chipping away until they can get pass the hardness and get to the heart of the individual. That's a unique ability. Maybe your passion is teaching children—I mean, you have the patience, temperament, ability to overcome the natural short attention spans of children, and the ability to articulate things in a way that children can really understand. That is also a unique gift, an indication that you thrive more in the area of communication with children.

Why seek out a career in a field where your purpose instincts don't apply? If you are not naturally drawn to something, you won't dedicate all of your time and energy to it. The place where you belong in life is the place that is best suited to utilize your natural instincts (talents, passions, and abilities). Some people were born to be engineers, some weren't; and some were born to be entrepreneurs while other are more suited for managerial and administrative roles. What are your instincts? And what things are you simply forcing yourself to do?

> If you are not naturally drawn to something, you won't dedicate all of your time and energy to it.

Knowing your instincts means knowing yourself, and knowing yourself is knowing who and what God made you and what you were designed by God to do in this world. All of it is tied up together. Knowing your purpose is connected to knowing the God-given "purpose instincts" you have. God places in us these instincts—or as the Bible puts it in one verse:

> "For God is working in you, giving you the desire and the power to do what pleases him." (Philippians 2:13, NLT)

There is a very simple principle at play here: When a person pursues after God, He'll cause them to desire what He predestined for them to have and do what He predestined for them to do. Here's the formula:

1. Develop a relationship with God

2. God places the right passions and desires in your heart

3. You pursue after those desires and passions and accomplish them.

Chapter 1: FOLLOW YOUR INSTINCTS

The problem is we treat God like an accessory. To us, He is just a fifth wheel that tags along just in case we run into an emergency and need a miracle. I'll show you how we treat God like an accessory:

- We don't pray first thing in the morning; we mainly pray when something bad happens.
- We don't ask the Holy Spirit to help us plan out our day before taking on the day; we just expect God to come to our rescue when our plans don't pan out.
- We don't focus on what God's will is for our lives; we only focus on what we want for ourselves and our lives, and then we expect God to make all of our self-centered plans come to pass.
- We don't give God the first portion of our increase (the tithe, which means "the first ten percent of our income/earnings) like the Bible tells us to do in Malachi 3:8-10; instead, we give God the scraps after we've paid off all of our bills and other expenses and have purchased all of the stuff we want.
- We don't read our Bibles; and therefore, we don't know what God expects of us in terms of how we

should live, behave, think, etc. Without knowing God's Word, we can't please Him and gain His favor, which we need for true success.

- We don't prioritize properly; and therefore, we'll place all of our attention on materialism and neglect our souls (Mark 8:36) and our relationships (why get all of the money in the world and lose your family in the process?).

These are a few examples of what we do wrong, and we wonder why the big picture is not clear to us. We wonder why it's so difficult for us to understand who we are and what we're supposed to be doing in life.

TOO MANY VOICES

It's not so much that God has to give us certain desires; it's actually that God has to redirect our focus to those things which He naturally embedded within us and predestined for us. Throughout life, we tend to get distracted and fall off course. We usually end up spending all of our time listening to people and what they want us to be and do, and in the process, we fail to listen to God and find out from Him what He wants us to be and do. We want to be what our parents want us to be, what our teachers want us to be, what the pastor wants us to be, what society tells us we should be; and ultimately, all of those voices are the distractions that prevent us from focusing on what God designed us to be.

We suppress our differences and proclivities in the presences of certain people—or all together—simply because others don't understand them. Some people call you weird for looking up at the stars each night. They call you a dreamer...as if there's anything wrong with that. Some people hate your confrontational personality. They call you a drama king/queen when in reality you just have the type of personality that gets things done and leaves no stone unturned. You don't avoid confrontation; you attack it. Leaders are people who attack problems before they become serious problems; they see what others don't see and address what others choose to ignore or deny. Every visionary is strange, weird, odd. Steve Jobs didn't see things the way others in his field saw things, and that is why he was fired from Apple Computers. But it's because of Steve Job's unique vision we have iphones and ipads and Apple watches today. People like Walt Disney were visionaries, but they were also ridiculed for their tendencies to zone out and get lost in their imaginations, sometimes during work. Many times they were accused of being unfocused when, actually, they were very focused—they were just focused on their dreams and employing their creativity, that which became the key ingredient in their successes later on in life. One young lady I met became hugely successful in the hair and make-up field, bringing in an income that trumped that which she was making in the financial field. Her parents called her crazy for leaving her accounting career behind just to do make-up, and they strongly criticized her for tossing away years of education for it. But her heart was in the beauty and fashion industry, and that's where all of her success, happiness and wealth came from. She was miserable while just sitting at a desk, staring at a screen, and crunching numbers all day. That was her parents' dream, not hers. But she lit up when she saw a Mack make-up store, and the mere sight of all the different make-up products caused her mind to soar and her creativity to stir.

Focus on your God-given instincts and spend time perfecting them, not listening to those who are trying to talk you out of pursuing them. Work on that job, but don't get comfortable. Even while on that 9 to 5, find time to examine your "purpose instincts". And don't let anyone make you feel ashamed of who you are and what makes you unique. Once you stop feeling ashamed of your proclivities, that's when you will gain the confidence to be what you were meant by God to be. You're a natural hunter. You were created to methodically pursue after dreams as if they are deer. The glory is in the hunt. That's why you will never be satisfied with sitting home doing nothing. You were made to hunt, to pursue, to conquer. There are dreams out there waiting on you. Go after them! Your time spent with God has fine-tuned your instincts, and now you've been released by God to be... YOU!!!

Follow *those* instincts.

STAY FOCUSED

CHAPTER 2
EMPLOY YOUR IMAGINATION

ONE OF THE MOST FASCINATING PASSAGES OF
Scripture in the Bible is Genesis 11:4-6. It is the
story of the Tower of Babel which was being built
by Nimrod and his followers just after the Flood of
Noah. It reads:

"And they said, Go to, let us build us a city

and a tower, whose top may reach unto heaven; and let us make us a name, lest we be scattered abroad upon the face of the whole earth. And the LORD came down to see the city and the tower, which the children of men builded. And the LORD said, Behold, the people is one, and they have all one language; and this they begin to do: and now nothing will be restrained from them, which they have imagined to do." (KJV)

It is interesting that God looked down from heaven and saw these people building a tower, and then got nervous. God got so nervous that He quickly rushed into action and confused the language of the people so that they couldn't finish their building project. By confusing the language, they were no longer able to communicate with one another, share their thoughts and ideas with each other, and work together. What were these people building that had God so nervous? It couldn't have simply been a regular skyscraper. We build skyscrapers all of the time today, and not once has God expressed concern over them. If God's fear was man's building of skyscrapers, then the Empire State Building in New York City and the Sear Tower in Chicago would've given God nightmares. But a skyscraper was not all these people were building. Nimrod wanted to build this tower as a symbol of defiance towards God, letting God know that mankind was united against Him and didn't need Him. But it wasn't Nimrod's motives that troubled God, it was the tower itself and the driving force behind it: In verse 6, God used the word "imagination" to describe the driving force behind this building project. Whatever Nimrod was attempting to build, it was something that sprung straight out of his evil imagination; something that was unnatural and even supernatural in nature; something that was extraordinary enough to impress even God. The point is this: What Nimrod imagined could actually be possible.

This passage of Scripture is an example of the power of the imagination. It reveals to us that things which we imagine can actually be created. Before we saw airplanes and jets, someone had to first imagine man soaring through the air like a bird. Before there was the invention of telephones by Alexander Graham Bell, someone had to imagine communicating over long distances instantly. Before all of the technology that we see today came into existence, it was first conceived in the imaginations of men. Men like

Thomas Edison, Nikola Tesla, Albert Einstein, and others first saw and envisioned the world we live in today—we're living out their imaginations.

Imagine transporting back through time with all of your current technological gadgets. What do you think, say, people living in the 14th century would think about your iphone, ipad, your vehicle, your laptop computer, your guns, your flashlight and other battery-powered devices, and even your clothing? They'd all be shocked, stunned, baffled, amazed, speechless, and think that you were either a deity or some space traveler from a faraway galaxy. Many of the things you currently take for granted would be EPIC to people living just a few decades, centuries, and millennia ago. So, don't assume that even the craziest, most far-fetched imaginative ideas today won't become realities tomorrow. With enough teamwork, time, progress and motivation, they can. God literally said they can when he declared that when a people become unified "nothing will be restrained from them, which they have imagined to do." Nothing!!

WHY THE IMAGINATION WORKS

What is the imagination? It is defined as "the ability

to form mental images of things that either are not physically present or have never been conceived or created by others." Mental pictures in the mind are powerful. Don't just say what you want to do in life, but picture what you want to do in life. Get a mental picture of yourself doing it in your mind. There's an element of power that images possess which words alone don't possess. Visual images are also able to motivate us in ways that words alone can't. There's an old saying: "A picture is worth a thousand words." Very true!

One of the reasons images are so powerful is because they, unlike words alone, don't leave much space for ambiguity. You can interpret something that is said many different ways. Even if a speaker is extremely articulate, there's still the possibility their words will get misinterpreted. A picture, on the other hand, is not as easy to misinterpret and twist around. Images are more encompassing in the communication process than words, allowing others to gain a

> Don't just say what you want to do in life, but picture what you want to do in life. Get a mental picture of yourself doing it in your mind.

complete, comprehensive understanding of what is

33

being communicated.

Why are images more effective than words when communicating with others? As science reveals to us, our brains don't "see words". When someone is speaking to you, your brain is not envisioning every alphabet used in every word that's coming out of the other person's mouth. No! Amazingly, your brain is actually busy trying to visualize everything the other person is saying. Why? Because the human brain can only see images, not words. So, this explains why showing a person a picture works better than just telling them what you want them to know. Their brain won't have to work as hard to "get the picture" when a picture is already being provided for them to see.

When we communicate with others we will quite often begin by saying things like "I want you to picture this" or "Imagine this" or "Let me describe something to you," and we will ask, "Do you see what I'm trying to say?" And when we understand what a person is saying, we usually respond by saying, "Oh, I see what you're saying." Communication is just the process of creating images in other people's minds. This is why television is so powerful: it creates images in the minds of the viewers. Great public speakers will usually use visual aids during their presentations and speeches, knowing that their effectiveness is determined by whether or not their audiences can

> Communication is just the process of creating images in other people's minds.

see what they're trying to convey in their speeches.

IMAGES IN THE SPIRITUAL REALM

Both God and Satan uses images. Every time Jesus would talk to the Jews, He'd use parables (short stories that carried a deeper message) to convey His truths. In each parable, Jesus relied heavily on imagery. He'd talk about seeds, tares, wheat, crops—you know, agricultural items. Why? Because most of the Jews at this time were farmers and shepherds. When Jesus spoke to Peter He talked about fish and fishing in order to get the message across to him. Why? It's because Peter was a fisherman by trade. Whenever Jesus wanted to get a message across, He'd do so using images people were familiar with. He knew that if the people could get a clear image of what He was saying in their minds, they could be "converted" and then "healed" (Matthew 13:13-15). God also relied heavily on images (imagery) when describing to the prophets Daniel and John what the end-times will look like.

The Bible says God will keep them "in perfect peace" whose "mind" (*yetser* in the Hebrew, meaning "imagination") stays on Him. 2 Corinthians 4:18 tells us to "look at things which are not seen", which involves utilizing the imagination to visualize things which God describes but have not yet manifested to the physical eyes. This is a simple definition of faith: Faith is the ability to visualize what God is telling us about our present and our future.

Satan uses what I call "anti-faith". Satan plays with our imaginations by causing us to visualize the wrong things and see ourselves in the wrong light.

> This is a simple definition of faith: Faith is the ability to visualize what God is telling us about our present and our future.

This is why the Bible tells us that Satan "blinds the minds" of people who reject Christ in 2 Corinthians 4:4, and why the Bible says we must use the power of God to "cast down thoughts and imaginations" in 2 Corinthians 10:4. Satan causes us to picture ourselves defeated. Most times, when we harbor fears in our lives, these fears are inspired by images we carry of ourselves being defeated, wronged, attacked, hurt, killed, losing someone close, having something very important taken or stolen from us, etc. First, we see an image in our minds of everyone else in the room looking at us funny and judging us, and then we get defensive and paranoid, thinking that other people are talking about us negatively. Every negative emotion starts with...a negative image that we carry in our minds. And the reality is those images aren't placed there by others; they are placed there by the enemy (Satan).

As a man thinks in his heart, so is he declares Solomon in Proverbs 23:7. The image in your mind will become your reality. The Bible repeatedly stresses to us to think about the good promises of God in the Old and New Testaments. This is what Paul said to do in Philippians 4:8. David told us to "meditate" on the Word and promises of God "day and night" in Psalm 1:2. This is so that our minds will constantly be filled with images of positive things like victory, miracles, healings, blessings, and our future glory in heaven. Why? So that we can carry a victorious and blessed attitude with us wherever we go, which will, in turn, transform the atmosphere around us. If you act defeated, you will create an atmosphere of defeat all around you and attract defeat to you. On the other hand, if you see yourself as victorious, you'll hold your head up and act victorious, which will cause the atmosphere around you to reflect victory. Whatever you think about the most, that will become your reality. So, God wants you to think about Him all day and all night so that you "give no place to the devil" (Ephesians 4:27) and make His blessings your reality in your daily living.

USE YOUR IMAGINATION

Now that you understand the power of the imagination, it's time to put it into context with regards to staying focused on your dreams and goals. Your imagination is the reflection of God's creative likeness in your life. God first envisioned a heaven and an earth in His mind, and then He spoke it into being. Likewise, whatever you want to do in life, you must first envision it in your mind, and then proceed from there to declare it with your mouth. If you can't first see it in your mind, you will never see it manifest before your eyes. God wants you to get a mental picture

> Whatever you think about the most, that will become your reality.

in your mind of what He's about to do. If faith is the only thing that moves God according to Hebrews 11:6, then you'd better get busy picturing and confessing every promise of God that He made to you about your life, and you'd better get busy seeing yourself

> If you can't first see it in your mind, you will never see it manifest before your eyes.

as a new creation rather than seeing yourself as the same old person that you use to be before getting saved. Don't just speak the blessing; see the blessing. See yourself financially prosperous. See yourself operating in that business. See yourself graduating from that school. See yourself receiving a standing ovation after giving that speech. See yourself being loved by someone and also loving someone. See yourself being a different person. See yourself being free from those bad habits. See yourself landing that job. See yourself driving that car and living in that house. See it! If God promised it to you, He did so in order that you might get a mental picture of you being that and doing that. The Bible says in 1 Corinthians 2:9-10,

"That is what the Scriptures mean when they

say, 'No eye has seen, no ear has heard, and no mind has imagined what God has prepared for those who love him.' But it was to us that God revealed these things by his Spirit. For his Spirit searches out everything and shows us God's deep secrets." (NLT)

God won't provide a visual image of His blessings to everyone. God specifically reveals these images to those who love Him, and He only reveals them to us by His Spirit (the Holy Spirit). So, know that those visions you've been having of yourself walking in all of these blessings I just mentioned are visions that have been given to you by God's Spirit. So, get busy visualizing them.

CHAPTER 3
CREATE AN ENVIRONMENT

CAN EASILY TELL HOW FOCUSED AND DISCIPLINED a person is and how successful they will be by looking at one thing: their environment. Yes! Your environment speaks volumes about you. What and who do you keep around you? What type of books are on your bookshelf at home? How do the walls in your house look? Do you have more televisions than you need or can count in your house? Etc.

There is an old saying: You are the company that you keep. This is true. What you choose to look at day after day will determine what you'll become in life. If you keep your eyes on mess, you'll become messy. If you look at junk day in and day out, your mind will only be filled with trashy thoughts. If you spend your time listening to vulgar and vile stuff on the radio and on television, you will think vulgar and vile thoughts day and night. If you feed your spirit a bunch of worldly stuff, you will find it difficult to get into the things of God and hear His voice. The Bible puts it this way:

> "Do not be deceived: God cannot be mocked. A man reaps what he sows. Whoever sows to please their flesh, from the flesh will reap destruction; whoever sows to please the Spirit, from the Spirit will reap eternal life." (Galatians 6:7-8, NIV)

Another Bible verse says,

> "Don't be fooled by those who say such things, for 'bad company corrupts good character.'"

Chapter 3: CREATE AN ENVIRONMENT

(1 Corinthians 15:33, NLT)

In both passages, the writer is urging us not to fool ourselves by believing that we can keep the wrong company and still prosper. That is being delusional. That is like sowing apple seeds and expecting to reap oranges. God is revealing to us a principle: Your environment determines your success or failure in life.

WRONG ENVIRONMENTS

There are certain environments that guarantee that you will fail. Here are a few:

Immoral Friends. Like you just read above, hanging around immoral people and individuals that have no goals or the wrong goals in life will cause you to lose sight of the right goals and develop the wrong goals in life as well. The company you keep determines the mentality you possess. Murderers, thieves, liars, criminals, and other such individuals hang together, and they all experience the same disastrous results in life: death, prison, shame, etc.. Visionaries, entrepreneurs, business owners, and successful people tend to hang together. Hanging with this kind of people will create a desire inside of you to be an entrepreneur, business owner, etc.

Negative People. Hanging around people who constantly speak negativity ("this will never work", "that won't work", "this can't be done", "you can't . . .") will dampen your soul and discourage you from pursuing your goals and dreams. Negativity will drain you gradually, zapping your energy until you can no longer feel excited about accomplishing what you initially set out to do. Now, don't confuse negativity with practicality. If a person is being practical by letting you know the challenges involved in a task or by giving you helpful advice with regards to what is the best way to go about accomplishing that goal, that is not the same as being negative. Also, if a person tells you not to do something that will jeopardize your soul and your life, they're not being negative either; instead, they're giving you advice that will save your life. The Bible says, "Wounds from a sincere friend are better than many kisses from an enemy" (Proverbs 27:6, NLT). Lastly, if a person gives you honest criticism as it pertains to something you've done or are doing, that is not the same as negativity either. We need critics, but we don't need cynics.

Chapter 3: CREATE AN ENVIRONMENT

Distractions. A man was telling my husband and me one day about an experience he had doing work for a Jewish family up in New York. He said that he had to go into the house to do some electrical work, and he noticed one thing: there were no televisions. One thing he said that really stood out to me was this: he stated, "Many Jewish families don't watch television, but they create and execute big ideas. But many of us have big televisions and small ideas." I thought about that for a moment. We have so many televisions we can't keep count—a television in each room, even the bathroom. All day long all we find ourselves staring at big TV screens, looking at TV programming that we've seen a million times, reality TV shows that keep us plugged into what someone else is doing rather than what we should be doing, and music videos that keep our minds filled with junk; and

yet, we always claim that we can't find the time to draw out a business plan, map out our lives, fellowship with the Holy Spirit and seek God for direction in life, come up with new business ideas and execute them, write that book, read, etc. It isn't that we don't have the time for these things; it's just that all of our time is being eaten up by distractions.

Television is good for certain purposes, and there are some television shows that are helpful for you, but the vast majority of the programming that comes on TV isn't helpful to us in any way. The more televisions and the bigger the screens, the less focused you are and the smaller your vision and ideas.

Today, there's another distraction to watch out for: social media (Facebook, Twitter, Instagram, etc.). Now, don't get me wrong. I love and appreciate social media. After all, I  do social media marketing. But when you spend all of your time looking at your timeline and keeping up with what other people are eating, drinking, doing, wearing, driving, etc., you'll discover that you're focusing less on what you need to be doing. It's easy to get caught-up into focusing on unimportant stuff on social media. It's easy to get so caught-up into social media that you even neglect your family (spouse, children, etc.) and allow the communication in those relationships to deteriorate. If you're going to use social media, use it for the right cause, one that is going to help your career, business, ministry, etc. Stop looking others' lives and focus on yours.

THINGS TO SURROUND YOURSELF WITH

Now that we've covered what not to have around you, let's cover what you need to place around you in order to stay focused:

Good Mentors, Coaches, and Supporters. Everyone needs a mentor, a coach, and a support system in life. Athletes depend on coaches to bring out the best in them. Businessmen and businesswomen depend on mentors to steer them in the right direction regarding their business decisions. Successful people know how to pull on the wisdom of others who have gone before them. The book of Proverbs repeatedly stresses to us the importance of listening to the voice of wisdom so that we don't repeat mistakes that could otherwise be avoided. Proverbs 15:22 says, "Plans go wrong for lack of advice; many advisers bring success" (NLT). Do you have a coach? A mentor? Are you teachable? Or are you too foolish to let someone mentor, coach and guide you, thinking that you can succeed on your own? Don't be foolish. Pray and ask God to send you to (or send to you) the right coach, mentor, and the right support group. Get connected with others who can provide wise counsel to you. It will save you time and headache and greatly improve your chances of not only remaining focused on your goals but executing them successfully.

Like-minded People. While seeking out to mentors and coaches, you also need to align yourself with like-minded people who will help you keep your eyes on your goals and also keep your mind stim-

ulated. You need to hang around people with big dreams. These type of people will cause you to dream bigger. If you only hang around people whose only desire in life is to make minimum wage at the local fast food restaurant, then your mind will remain at that level. If you hang around people who dream of being CEOs and business owners and professionals, they'll entice you to pursue bigger plans. Other dreamers will help you to dream, and visionaries will inspire you to get a vision for yourself. Leaders will teach you how to lead. You should have a team of people with different gifts, abilities, insights, talents and expertises. As the Bible declares: "As iron sharpens iron, so a friend sharpens a friend" (Proverbs 27:17, NLT). Just don't get envious or jealous of your teammates gifts. Know that everyone isn't supposed to have the same

> Wisdom causes you to link up with the individuals who have what you don't possess, not try to out-do, out-shine and compete with them. That's foolish, and that's a recipe for failure.

gifts and abilities. Wisdom causes you to link up with the individuals who have what you don't possess, not try to out-do, out-shine and compete with them. That's foolish, and that's a recipe for failure. Deal with your insecurities by understanding your value and worth in the sight of God and knowing what His purpose is for your life. Focus on that and you won't become jealous of others. He has a plan for you. He has a set time for your blessings to come.

He holds the future in His hands, not other people. And He made you for His purpose, and not your own (Proverbs chapter 16).

Visual Cues. You need to surround yourself with visual cues that keep you reminded and inspired from day to day. Scientifically, there are certain things that marketers use to grow their businesses and generate more sales. Simple things that most people overlook are some of the biggest things that make a difference in marketing. For example, colors are strongly used by restaurants. Research has discovered that certain colors evoke feelings of hunger. Red and yellow are two of the main colors. So, take notice of how many fast food restaurants you see that have a red and/or yellow color scheme. Certain images coupled with certain sounds tend to appeal to our subconscious minds. Advertisers know the importance of keeping certain images before your eyes on the television screens through commercials. They know that after you've been exposed to a certain image for a certain number of times it will unconsciously resonate within you. Have you ever found yourself singing a little jingle from a commercial without realizing it? Well, that commercial (its imagery, sounds, message and more) is unconsciously playing in your mind so that when you walk into a store filled with thousands of products your eyes will actually take notice of that one product that was advertised on that commercial.

What cues are you setting up around you in order to unconsciously set yourself up for success? I noticed that my husband would create cues for himself to keep himself motivated. For example, while working on a book, he would always create the cover for that book first and then use that cover as his screen-saver on his computer at his job, his laptop, his ipad, and even his cell phone; that way, every time he opened up his laptop computer, sat at his desk at work, and picked up his cellphone he was reminded of the book he was writing. It may have seemed like an obsession, but it wasn't; it was just the Law of Focus being applied.

For myself, I discovered that I needed to keep visual cues around my home to inspire me. I created a Vision Board and placed it right next to my bed so that each night I would see it—I would see all of my plans, goals, and dreams—and be reminded of where I'm going in life and what I'm supposed to be doing with my time. I put up artwork around my house in certain sections so that my creative juices would be stirred. There is a reason why art is so important: it unconsciously evokes emotions, passion, and stirs up the creativity in our souls.

Another thing that my husband does is play music whenever he's working on a project. He loves to listen to classical and instrumental music because it stimulates his mind. Music evokes emotions, but some emotions aren't healthy for you; therefore, you must be cautious of the type of music you listen to.

Decorate your house with artwork and colors. These things will stir up the creative juices within you and help your thoughts flow more fluidly.

Lastly, keep little sticky notes around to keep yourself reminded of certain tasks. Write notes to yourself; place remind-ers on your cell phone, laptops, computers, ipads, and other devices that remind you of things you need to do. Keep a journal by your bed at night and journal your goals, dreams and the steps that you need to take to accomplish those goals and dreams. Make sure that you create an environment that inspires and reminds you to focus on your goals and dreams.

CHAPTER 4
DETOX YOUR LIFE

Y̶OU CAN TELL WHEN YOUR BODY NEEDS A DETOX. You feel sluggish, your energy levels are low, you feel constipated, depressed, overweight, have a hard time sleeping, and even suffer from headaches, sexual dysfunction, and allergies. But one big indication that you need to detox your body is the inability to... focus. When your body is filled with too much toxic waste, it begins to affect your brain function. This is

53

a big source of the brain-fog that many people suffer with.

Be mindful of your physical health. It is tied to your mental and emotional health. Sometimes, a person is suffering from depression, not because of a demon or negative circumstance, but because they just won't get up off of the couch and exercise and also detoxify their body. Your body is the temple of the Holy Spirit; take care of it, value it, keep it clean and don't waste it. Don't get so caught up in working on projects and other things that you neglect to take care of your body and keep your health up. If you let your health go down you won't have the energy and the strength to do those projects you're trying to get done and pursue those dreams that you have. Losing your health is like having your car to break down on you while you're in a rush to get somewhere important. You don't want that.

Not to spend a lot of time on this, but I want to give a few quick tips on detoxing your body: try to eat organic foods, exercise (sweating releases toxins out of your body), get a message, drink more water, eat lots of fiber, and drink detox smoothies and teas. Do this for a short period of time and you'll feel the difference in your body, energy levels and your mind.

Chapter 4: DETOX YOUR LIFE

ARE YOU A HOARDER?

Now that we got that out of the way, let's move on to something even more pressing when it comes to the issue of staying focused: clutter. Clutter occurs when a person has too much stuff in their personal space. A house can be cluttered. There are people who are known as hoarders. These people never throw things away. Their houses look like dumpsites.

The above photo is an example of a hoarder's house. Notice how cluttered it is. This is a person who just can't let go of old stuff. They live in the past and in a state of fear, afraid that if they were to part with a single item they would only be throwing away something that they will later need up the road. In many cases, they've attached a strong sentimental value to objects and they just can't let them go.

No one would want to visit such a house. No one in their right mind would dare live in that kind of environment. You'd be afraid to sit down for fear of sitting on something sticky, sharp, or something alive and poisonous. You can't see your way through that type of environment. Quite frankly, it's gross; it is disturbing to even look at.

Now picture this: This is how our minds look when they're cluttered. Internally, we look filthy and unsanitary, dangerous and atrocious; we are uninviting, unattractive, and fogged-up; light barely penetrates the darkness of our souls.

No one, after visiting a house like this, would ask the homeowner for help, guidance, or to partner with them in business; instead, they would be more inclined to offer to get them some professional help. And the same goes for our lives. When our lives are too cluttered, we're in no position to help others. We need help. And only after we've clean-up our houses are we capable of helping others. We have to get rid of the old junk from our pasts. We have to forgive and release the offenses clamored in our hearts that we've been carrying for so long. People can tell when you are carrying offenses in your heart, despite all of the fake smiles and the facade you wear. When your mind is cluttered your past and your present offenses will seep out in your interactions with others. You will judge others, take out your problems on others, become overly defensive, sensitive and easily offended. People will be able to tell that you're filled with a lot of...junk. It will make you very unappealing.

When your mind is cluttered you can't think or be creative. Clutter blocks your thoughts. If you're cluttered you will find it difficult just to concentrate on the tasks before you. Oftentimes, the biggest distractions aren't the ones around us, but the ones within us. Not taking the time to get healed from emotional wounds will only hinder us from focusing on our goals and dreams.

> When your mind is cluttered you can't think or be creative. Clutter blocks your thoughts.

Not only does unforgiveness lead to cluttered minds, but also worry, anxiety and fear will cause us to be filled with mental clutter. These emotions all stem from the belief that we are in control of everything. In essence, the person who lives in a state of anxiety and fear is the person who hasn't learned how to let go and trust God. Being a control-freak keeps us in a state of worry. We think that we are *god* enough to be everywhere at one time, prevent every bad thing from happening, protect and provide for everyone in the world, do everything for everyone, make everyone happy, meet everyone's needs, and be everyone's savior. We forget that there is only one Savior: Jesus the Christ. We forget that there's only one God: His name is God Jehovah. He's the only omniscient and omnipotent being who sees everything. He possesses infinite wisdom and has the ultimate plan. Unless we learn how to pray for others and trust

> ...the person who lives in a state of anxiety and fear is the person who hasn't learned how to let go and trust God.

them into God's hands, we will always allow their worries to become our worries and their issues to clutter our lives. Do what you can to help, but don't worry about doing that which you can't do. Let people get angry or upset with you. They have to learn how to call upon the Lord for themselves just like you have to. You're not their god.

Chapter 4: DETOX YOUR LIFE

DE-CLUTTERING YOUR LIFE

Here are a few steps to take to de-clutter your life:

Clean and organize your living space. A cluttered mind leads to a cluttered life, and our environments reflect what's going on inside of us. When your house is clean, the open space tends to have a trickle-down effect on your thinking, causing your mind to feel a lot less cluttered as well. That simple act of reorganizing your closet, reorganizing your bedroom, your living room, your den; that simple act of cleaning up your home will lift your spirit psychologically. Try it! Try it at home, at work, and in your car! If not, then the sight of a cluttered living space will continue to add to the clutter that's already in your mind.

Stop living in the past. This is easier said than done, but it is not only possible, it's necessary that we step out of yesterday and into the present. Stop worrying about the future and focus on the daily tasks that are sitting right in front of you. Some people can't seem to get started today because of they're worried about the future—whether or not they'll fail. Let go of all of

> A cluttered mind leads to a cluttered life...

these thoughts and just jump into the moment. If you failed before in the past, don't assume that you'll experience the same results this time. Most successful people have failed multiple times while pursuing a dream, but they're successful simply because...they didn't let failure stop them. They kept going. Do like the Apostle Paul in the Bible, who wrote,

> "No, dear brothers and sisters, I have not achieved it, but I focus on this one thing: Forgetting the past and looking forward to what lies ahead..." (Philippians 3:13, NLT)

Let yesterday's victories and failures be yesterday's victories and failures. Today is a new day! Jesus told us to focus on the day at hand in Luke 12:22-31. In James 4:13-16, God declares,

> "Look here, you who say, 'Today or tomorrow we are going to a certain town and will stay there a year. We will do business there and make a profit.' How do you know what your life will be like tomorrow? Your life is like the morning fog—it's here a little while, then it's gone. **What you ought to say is, 'If the Lord**

wants us to, we will live and do this or that.'
Otherwise you are boasting about your own
plans, and all such boasting is evil."

Make talking to God a habit and a regular practice
of yours. Ask Him for the wisdom to navigate the
challenges throughout that day. Also, ask Him for
His guidance in planning for the next day and all of
the days ahead. Let Him guide you.

Spend time with God first thing in the morning. It is
crucial that you start your day with God, worship-
ing and praising Him and entering into His presence before you set-out to do anything and tackle
anything the day has to bring. When you enter into
the presence of the Lord first thing in the morning,
you will find your soul being lifted, fear and anxiety
dissolving, courage and strength arising within, and
you'll also put your-
self in a position to
hear the voice of
the Holy Spirit as
He begins to speak
to you and give you
instructions for that

> Make talking to God a habit and
> a regular practice of yours. Ask
> Him for the wisdom to navigate
> the challenges throughout that
> day.

day. The Bible tells us that there is peace, joy, assurance, divine confidence, protection, and deliverance from mental torment in the presence of the Lord. You need these things before you take on the day and get faced with all of the worldly cares, pressures, stresses . . . and the spiritual attacks waiting to hit you.

Spending time with God, reading His Word and meditating on it throughout the day, and praising Him throughout the day, will take your mind off of all of the wrong things and set your day in order. In order to establish a new habit, researchers tell us we must do something consistently for 21 days. Try entering into the presence of God through worship every morning and meditating on the Word of God consistently for the next 21 days. See how you'll feel after that. Notice how your mind will have changed, negative emotions would have disappeared, and you will have gained a different perspective—a far better one—in life. God will also heal you of your pain and hurts from the past and teach you how to forgive as He forgives.

Remember: True prosperity, as defined by in the Word of God in 3 John 1:2, is when you're prospering not just financially, but spiritually as well.

CHAPTER 5
THE GATES TO YOUR SOUL

ONE OF THE MOST IMPORTANT PRINCIPLES THAT I can stress to you is the importance of protecting your eyes and your ears. Your eyes and your ears are the entrances to your soul, and what goes into your soul is what controls your thoughts, actions and life.

The Bible tells us to protect our hearts at all cost. Prosperity begins with the heart (soul). 3 John

1:2 tells us that our physical prosperity will come as our souls prosper. This is important because it is our thoughts and beliefs that create our realities; therefore, if you want to change your life you must begin by changing your mentality—we covered this in the previous chapters.

The Bible says,

"Guard your heart above all else, for it determines the course of your life." (Proverbs 4:23, NLT)

What goes into your heart determines what direction your life goes in. Allow mess in your heart and your life will end-up messy. Allow jealousy and envy in your heart and you'll always find yourself feeling insecure and less than others, and will therefore miss opportunities to advance in your own life because of your insecurities. If you allow the love of God to fill your heart you will find your life heading in a direction of purpose, meaningfulness, righteousness, and extraordinary blessings. If you allow God's wisdom and humility to fill your heart, you will find yourself being elevated to success and great favor with men as explained in 1 Peter 5:5-6 which says,

"In the same way, you younger men must accept the authority of the elders. And all of you, serve each other in humility, for 'God opposes the proud but favors the humble.' So humble yourselves under the mighty power of God, and at the right time he will lift you up in honor."

The biggest caution concerning our hearts comes from Jesus who said in Luke 12:15,

"Then he said, 'Beware! Guard against every kind of greed. Life is not measured by how much you own.'" (NASB)

Society teaches people to be greedy. We are groomed from our childhood up to determine our value based off of the material possessions we have; and as a result of this, we spend all of our time pursuing after worldly possessions just so that we can prove to others that we're important. We tell our children to go to school so that they can get a good job and make a lot of money, and we emphasize strongly that if they don't obtain these things they will be seen as failures in life. You'll be viewed as a nobody if you don't have a big car, big house, and a big bank account. By this standard, if your car is smaller than another's or your house is smaller than another's, then your value as a person is less than another's. This is known as being materialistic; or as Jesus put it, this is being *covetous* (being an "idolater," which is a person who worships someone or something other than the true and living God according to Colossians 3:5).

This way of thinking produces several negative attitudes within us: **pride** (we assume that we're self-sufficient and don't need anyone else, including God); **arrogance** (we believe we're better than other people); **selfishness** (meaning "lacking consideration for others; concerned chiefly with one's own personal profit or pleasure"); and lastly, **discontentment** (dissatisfaction with one's own circumstances). All of these attitudes guarantee one thing: God will not only *not* bless us, but He will fight against us as 1 Peter 5:5 tells us. And don't worry about people who seem to be prospering right now although they have the wrong attitude because, according to Psalm 37, their prosperity is short-lived and after they die hell is their portion (Mark 10:25).

Your life on this earth is temporary, only

lasting for a brief period of time. We're all going to die one day, but the question is this: When you die, will your soul be prepared to stand before God? Will you be allowed to enter into heaven, or will you hear God say to you, "Depart from me. I never knew you"? According to the Bible, if you spend all of your time pursuing the world and worldly things, you'll not make it into the Kingdom of Heaven. The Bible says this about chasing after the world:

> "Do not love this world nor the things it offers you, for **when you love the world, you do not have the love of the Father in you.**" (1 John 2:15, NLT)

> "You adulterers! **Don't you realize that friendship with the world makes you an enemy of God?** I say it again: If you want to be a friend of the world, you make yourself an enemy of God." (James 4:4, NLT)

> "Those who are dominated by the sinful nature think about sinful things, but those who are controlled by the Holy Spirit think about things that please the Spirit. **So letting**

your sinful nature control your mind leads to death. But letting the Spirit control your mind leads to life and peace. For the sinful nature is always hostile to God. It never did obey God's laws, and it never will. That's why those who are still under the control of their sinful nature can never please God." (Romans 8:5-8, NLT)

"Don't be misled—you cannot mock the justice of God. You will always harvest what you plant. Those who live only to satisfy their own sinful nature will harvest decay and death from that sinful nature. But those who live to please the Spirit will harvest everlasting life from the Spirit." (Galatians 6:7-8, NLT)

The Bible is clear: Live for the world and you'll miss heaven. It doesn't matter how popular, famous, rich, and admired you are by men; if your eyes are on the things of the world rather than the will of God, you will end-up in the flames of hell. There are going to be a lot of celebrities who were well

> The Bible is clear: Live for the world and you'll miss heaven.

loved and cherished by men in hell. There will be a lot of rich and powerful people in hell. There will be a lot of people in general in the flames of hell according to Jesus in Matthew 7:13-14. Why? It's because many people are focused only on their lives on earth, but they're neglecting the state of their souls—they aren't living for God, but rather, for themselves. They don't want to live obediently to God and serve Him with their lives. And in response to this, Jesus stated,

> "And what do you benefit if you gain the whole world but lose your own soul?" (Mark 8:36, NLT)

With this comes a key Law of Focus principle: Stop looking at the majority, trying to do the same things that they're doing, and realize that the majority can easily be on the wrong track. If you want to succeed in God's will and plan for your life, be prepared to be exceptional and stand-out from the crowd; get ready to walk alone, following only God's voice.

> Law of Focus principle: Stop looking at the majority, trying to do the same things that they're doing, and realize that the majority can easily be on the wrong track.

STAY FOCUSED

When your heart has been corrupted by the world's beliefs, you'll find yourself focused on the things of the flesh and will miss God, your purpose in life, and heaven after you die. You will find yourself being derailed from your purpose, which is your reason for existing. Don't be misled.

UNGRATEFUL POTATO HEAD

Many people are angry today despite having all of the blessings in the world. They just can't seem to be satisfied with what they have. If your life is driven by greed, then you will never be satisfied. You can have a million dollars in your bank account, and still, you will be desirous of having a million and one dollars. You can have everything you need but still can't enjoy any of it. That is misery. You're forever unhappy. You're always ungrateful. You're always anxious. You are always feeling empty inside. This is how a lot of celebrities and wealthy people feel—I'm speaking of those who have material wealth, but not a relationship with Christ which leads to an understanding of their purpose in life. The world breeds discontentment in us by making

> If your life is driven by greed, then you will never be satisfied.

us greedy. This is a deception. The Bible says in 1 Timothy 6:5-10,

> "These people always cause trouble. Their minds are corrupt, and they have turned their backs on the truth. To them, a show of godliness is just a way to become wealthy. **Yet true godliness with contentment is itself great wealth. After all, we brought nothing with us when we came into the world, and we can't take anything with us when we leave it.** So if we have enough food and clothing, let us be content. **But people who long to be rich fall into temptation and are trapped by many foolish and harmful desires that plunge them into ruin and destruction. For the love of money is the root of all kinds of evil. And** some people, craving money, have wandered from the true faith and pierced themselves with many sorrows." (1 Timothy 6:5-10, NLT)

If you can't be content with where you are, noticing the blessings you already have and expressing thanks to God for them now, you'll be discontent, miserable and unhappy always. Remember: God doesn't bless spoiled and ungrateful people. Don't become greedy, spoiled, ungrateful, selfish, bitter and miserable. And don't become desperate to enter into the world's rat race and accumulate material possessions while your soul is in jeopardy. Placing your focus on the money will cause you to wonder from God and fill your life with "many sorrows" up the road. Being greedy and chasing only after more money will derail you from your purpose and jeopardize everything. Greed will impair your judgment. No! You're never making the right decision when money is your motivation. Your actions will always lead to disaster. Solomon wrote:

> You're never making the right decision when money is your motivation.

"Don't wear yourself out trying to get rich. Be wise enough to know when to quit. In the blink of an eye wealth disappears, for it will sprout wings and fly away like an eagle." (Proverbs 23:4-5, NLT)

"Wealth from get-rich-quick schemes quickly disappears; wealth from hard work grows over time." (Proverbs 13:11, NLT)

Be patient and not greedy. Learn how to be content.

HOW TO GUARD YOUR HEART/SOUL

How do you guard your heart, your soul? You do so by monitoring what you hear and what you see. The Bible tells us in 1 John 2:16,

> "For the world offers only a craving for physical pleasure, a craving for everything we see, and pride in our achievements and possessions. These are not from the Father, but are from this world." (NLT)

Whatever you look at the most, that will be what you focus on the most. If you look at everyone else's lives, you'll be distracted from the life God is calling you to live. If you keep your eyes on people, you will never hear what God is saying to you about you. If you look at pornography all day, your mind will constantly be filled with lustful thoughts and you'll find it difficult to build healthy relationships. If you look at violent movies all day, you'll find your mind filled with violent images on a constant basis. If you look at demonic things, you'll find yourself being plagued by demonic thoughts (darkness, death, suicide, fear, torment, violence, etc.). If you look at immoral people, you will find yourself being drawn to their lifestyles. If you keep your eyes on God, you will walk in His wisdom, understanding, prosperity, and peace.

Don't just monitor what you watch with your eyes, but also monitor what you hear with your ears. The Bible says, "Faith comes by hearing, and hearing by the Word of God" in Romans 10:17. If you listen to people who speak doubt, you'll doubt what God says about you. If you listen to people who only talk about ungodly things, then your mind will only be filled with ungodly and worldly thoughts (1 Corinthians 15:33; 2 Timothy 2:16). You can't get focused on what God will have you to do if you're constantly listening to worldly things. So, here are a few things you need to do now to get focused or refocused:

- Fast (turn down the plate, turn off the television and radio, and just pray and read God's Word).
- Find quiet time each day to spend with God
- Avoid negative and sinful conversations. When people come to you with mess, redirect their attention to God by offering to pray about things

as opposed to engaging in gossip.
• Hang around people of faith (Malachi 3:13-17).

Remember to keep mess out of your heart and keep your heart clean. If mess has gotten into your heart, then pray this simple prayer:

> **Lord Jesus, I pray that You create in me a clean heart and give me the right spirit today. Let me focus on Your will for my life today so that I may please You. Forgive me of my sins even as I forgive others. I thank you, in Jesus name. Amen.**

STAY FOCUSED

CHAPTER 6
FIND YOUR BALANCE

$\mathcal{S}$OMETIMES, LIFE CAN OVERWHELM YOU. IF YOU don't be careful, you can find yourself buried underneath an avalanche of responsibilities without having any room to breathe. Being overwhelmed is never good; it places a lot of stress on your body, and it wears you down physically and mentally. When a person finds him or herself overwhelmed, it's always due to the fact that they have gotten out of balance in their life. And no, this isn't a form of living life on the edge; this is a form of living life under unnecessary stress, pressure, and anxiety, which is unhealthy and foolish.

Aside from running my own business, teaching Bible Study weekly, holding prayer calls weekly, conducting a weekly prayer service at 5 am; speaking publicly in churches, schools, and other venues; putting on yearly events and more, I am also a wife and a mother of three (two boys and a girl). I still model and do acting. I do a lot of things. I find it important to be able to pace myself and balance everything less I become overwhelmed. Oh, and I didn't even mention the fact that I have not only my family pulling on me but friends and other colleagues that pull on me, looking for my support at their many events and activities.

> When a person finds him or herself overwhelmed, it's always due to the fact that they have gotten out of balance in their life.

How do I balance all of this? How do I make it throughout the day without losing my mind? How do I deal with the flood of demands that pour in day after day? Well, I'll show you in these few easy steps:

Chapter 6: FIND YOUR BALANCE

Write out your day. Do you have a planner? Do you have a notebook that you record your tasks and the steps that you have to take to accomplish them in? One of the most important parts of strategizing is writing all of your goals, tasks, and responsibilities down and then committing to following a schedule. It's important that you establish new habits that will set you up to focus on the things you need to. One of the most important habits you can ever establish is a habit of planning out your day, and planning should always be done in writing...so you won't forget.

Prioritize. It is so important that you first prioritize before making any decisions in your life. Take a look at your life and figure out what should be a priority in your life, taking precedent above all else. If you just sit back and tackle everything that arises as it comes and don't rank things on a scale of what's important and what's less important, you will find yourself spending valuable time on things that aren't really important and critical while neglecting to do those things that must be done right away. For example, my priorities are (listed from the highest to least): God, family, my health, and then my business and ministry obligations come, followed by helping and supporting my extended family members, friends, colleagues, and others.

God comes first. I have to pray and acknowledge God before I start my day. Many mornings I'll lie in the bed with my eyes shut and pray. I may get up and grab my devotionals and read a little. After I speak to God in the morning, I'll focus on meeting my husband's *needs*, knowing that this is important both for him and pleasing in God's eyes according to 1 Corinthians 7:5, which says of married couples,

> "Do not deprive each other of sexual relations, unless you both agree to refrain from sexual intimacy for a limited time so you can give yourselves more completely to prayer. Afterward, you should come together again so that Satan won't be able to tempt you because of your lack of self-control." (NLT)

Taking care of my responsibilities in the home is a top priority of mine because it is what God ranks as being highly important. 1 Timothy 5:8 says,

> "But those who won't care for their relatives,

especially those in their own household, have denied the true faith. Such people are worse than unbelievers." (NLT)

God wants us to prioritize according to His Word, not according to man's opinions. And according to God, focusing on the needs of the family and building strong relationships in the home is key to securing His divine favor over our other endeavors in life. In the morning times, my husband and I usually take a little time to discuss our goals, planning and strategizing—he'll share ideas with me and I'll share ideas with him. We strategize on where the money will go and what projects we'll focus on first. We understand the importance of the two of us being on one accord. Next, I prioritize my health. I make sure to eat right and keep my children healthy also—dealing with

> ...according to God, focusing on the needs of the family and building strong relationships in the home is key to securing His divine favor over our other endeavors in life.

all kinds of sicknesses can be both financially draining and time-consuming. Practice preventative measures as opposed to reactionary measures. What I mean by that is build up your kids' immune systems before the winter months; eat healthily and exercise before a serious health scare arises (high blood, diabetes, etc.) and steals your money and time. Next, I make sure to take care of any business and ministry obligations that I have at that time. I have arrangements made ahead of time for someone to take care of the kids so that I may fulfill my obligations without distraction. I then attempt to help others through physical and financial means only after my house is taken care of. Any money that need to be spent on my household doesn't go to family and friends, no matter how bad and how much they beg, grumble and complain. My time spent with family takes precedent over the time spent with others; therefore, if my husband wants us to go out on a date at the same time that someone else wants me to support their event, I will prioritize my date night above the other person's event. And if my husband and I don't have anything planned for the evening and someone else wants my support, I'll then give it to them . . . if I'm not too tired.

Budget. So many people do things without looking at their finances first. Now, I am a person of faith. I believe in walking by faith, but I also know what the meaning of walking by faith is: it means listening to God's instructions, not taking foolish, unnecessary and unadvised risks based off of your feelings. God has given us instructions in His Word concerning money already. Proverbs 6:6-8 tells us to follow the example of the ant who works in the summer in order to save up for the winter—a time when no work can be done. Solomon calls those who refuse to plan adequately and properly for the winter months of their lives "sluggards" (lazybones).

It is ungodly to waste money and then expect for God to simply perform a financial miracle when the need comes. God instructs us to be good stewards over our possessions in Luke 16:11. Plainly put, if we can't manage what we already have, then God can't bless us with more. We have to demonstrate to God that we are capable of managing the little that we have before asking for more (Luke 16:10-12).

Many people get angry at wealthy people for having so much, but the Bible makes it clear that you shouldn't look at another person's blessings and envy them; instead, you should look at what that person did in order to get what they have. Look at the story behind the glory. Proverbs 21:20 says,

"The wise have wealth and luxury, but fools spend whatever they get." (NLT)

Also, Proverbs 21:17 says,

"Those who love pleasure become poor; those who love wine and luxury will never be rich." (NLT)

Lastly, Proverbs 22:7 declares,

"Just as the rich rule the poor, so the borrower is servant to the lender." (NLT)

Notice the causes of financial ruin, which also leads to ruin in so many other areas of our lives (marriage, business, ministry, family, etc.): excessive spend-  ing, addictions to alcohol and other substances, and excessive borrowing.

Before you talk about starting another business, pay off the debts you currently have. Before you talk about taking out another loan, pay off the one(s) you currently have. Before you talk about pursuing a dream in business, get help for the addictions you're wrestling with now. Don't think for one minute that money and success are going to automatically cure you of your addictions or even improve the quality of your life; money and success might end up making your situation worse. Control your impulse to spend money "just because you have it," and practice self-control. If you can't control your impulse to buy and spend then even if you get a promotion on your job you'll still be in debt because as your income increases so will your spending; and as your spending increases, so will your debt.

If you don't understand how to manage money, you will always be broke. Before seeking to gain money, buy books and get the information needed to help you understand how to properly handle and manage money. As the Bible says, "In all thy getting get understanding" (Proverbs 4:7).

> If you can't control your impulse to buy and spend then even if you get a promotion on your job you'll still be in debt because as your income increase so will your spending...

Part of the budgeting process is planning for events ahead of time.

Don't wait until they are right upon you to scramble to try to find money. Prepare months in advance. Save up money gradually. Put a little money on the side out of each paycheck—this is emergency money or money for an event or activity. Add up the total amount of money that you get for the month and match that with the total amount of your monthly expenses. If your expenses are more than your income intake, then it's time to cut some of those expenses, starting with the things you can do without or do yourself. For example, if you have to do your own hair for a while, do it. If you have to learn how to fix things around the house, learn how to do it yourself so you can save money. If you don't need so many cable channels, then get a cheaper cable plan/subscription.

> If your expenses are more than your monthly income intake, then it's time to cut some of those expenses...

Cut-off lights in rooms where you're not so you can save money on the light bill. If you can do your own nails, do them. If you've been spending a lot of money on clothes, stop it and apply that money to your savings. I hate to say it, but you have to downgrade your quality of living sometimes. You have to learn

86

to live beneath your means. Don't worry about impressing anyone. Start saving money for your rainy days while keeping in mind that those same people you are trying to impress won't be there to bail you out when you fall.

Multi-task less. Everyone loves to look busy. But looking busy and getting stuff done are two different things. Many people look busy, but they aren't actually accomplishing anything. Getting things done is a matter of prioritizing, managing one's time and focusing all of one's attention on one thing at a time. Research has shown that those who focus on too many things at one time tend not to get much, if anything, done. Focusing on several tasks at one time may cause us to neglect other tasks or miss important details pertaining to certain tasks. Try ironing clothes while both cooking breakfast and typing a report at the same time— you'll more than likely end up

burning the breakfast, or a hole in your clothes, or making errors on your report, if not all three.

There's an old saying: A jack of all trades is a master of none. When you try to be good at everything you end up being mediocre at best at everything. Most successful people in life gained success not because they were good at everything, but because they were good at one thing and they focused all of their attention on doing just that. Tyler Perry, one of the most successful and famous playwrights in the world, told his story about how for nearly ten years he held on to his dream and never lost sight of it—he clung onto his "purpose instincts". He talked about how when he first started producing plays, no one would show up. He would take his income tax return money and finance his plays on his own. He could have given up and placed his sights on something else, but he didn't. He knew playwriting was his calling; it was his passion. Years later after he started his journey, he finally hit success. *Madea*, his stage play, be-

> Most successful people in life gained success not because they were good at everything, but because they were good at one thing and they focused all of their attention on doing just that.

came a hit and a media sensation. His success with *Madea* opened up the door for him to produce and star in movies, create his own sitcoms and television shows for television, create his own movie studio, and venture into several other business ventures, thereby opening up many other streams of income. But it all started with one thing: his passion; the one thing he knew he was called to do; the one thing he was good at. He didn't try to focus on several things; he only poured all of his time and energy into perfecting one craft.

What is the one thing you're called to do? What is the one thing that sets you apart from everyone else? What is your passion? Are you focusing on that? Or are you trying to do too many things at one time out of impatience, fear, and anxiety?

Manage your time. Defeat your tendency to procrastinate. Make a list of the tasks you have for the day, and then take care of the most important and most difficult tasks early in the day while your body and mind are both fresh and rested. Tackle these tasks early while you have the most energy and the least amount of mental clutter. As the day progresses, your mind will become more cluttered. You don't want to tackle challenging tasks while your mind isn't clear—while it's already bogged down with too much other stuff.

If you're anything like me—a busy mom who does several things—then it is important to be pro-

> **Make a list of the tasks you have for the day, and then take care of the most important and most difficult tasks early in the day while your body and mind are both fresh and rested.**

active and knock out the tasks that will free up more time in your day. Prepare the kid's clothes the night before so that you won't have to scramble to find something for them to wear in the morning. Prepare meals ahead of time so that food will be prepared for the household ahead of time. Most importantly, be flexible enough with your planning to include those unforeseen events. If you know the kids have to be up at 7 am for school, get up at 6:30 am to pray and read your Bible. To get up earlier, then you need to go to bed a little earlier. Make the necessary adjustments so that you can include the things which are necessary into your day. Strategize! You can't control life; you can only prepare for the unexpected.

Section off your time: time for personal business; me-time; work time; time to plan and discuss business; time to entertain phone calls from others (some people will spend up all of your personal and family time with their concerns and issues. My husband had to teach me how to make people respect my time. Only in the case of an emergency or something really important should you sacrifice personal time. But some matters can wait until the next day).

Sit down and write out a schedule for yourself. On your list, time spent with God should be at the top. After that, fill in the blanks with the things that are important—from the most to the least. Sit down and analyze your current use of time by examining your routine. If you notice that you spend too much time on non-important and wasteful things, then brainstorm and think of productive things you could replace those non-important things with.

Learn to say no. It isn't a sin or a crime to tell some people "no" or "not right now". It won't mentally and emotionally damage your child for life if you say no when they ask to go somewhere or buy something that they see right then and there. Buy saying no to your child, you'll be teaching them that they cannot have whatever they want whenever they want it, and this is a form of self-control that will help them later on in life. If you can't do it, you just can't do it. If you don't have the time to devote to it, you just don't have the time to devote to it, plain and simple. Don't sacrifice the most important relationships in your life just to get an extra dollar or two. Anyone that can't respect your values and what's important to you is someone you shouldn't try to please. People should know that there are some lines you won't cross, some things you won't try, certain principles you hold near and dear and won't compromise, and certain traditions you won't part with. If it is a family tradition to go bowling once a month, or vacation every year around a certain time, etc., then there is nothing wrong with establishing these facts in other people's minds so they'll know not to bother you for anything around those times. Stop giving in to everyone's demands; for, if you don't stop doing this, your life will always remain unbalanced.

Don't be afraid to ask for help. It doesn't matter how disciplined you are, you're going to need help if you are going to keep things in balance. A good boss is a person who knows how to delegate responsibility to others, not one that tries to do everything him or herself. The most successful leaders and business-men and businesswomen focus a great deal of their time building teams and perfecting the art of teamwork, not try-ing to shine like su-perstars. Make one of your biggest skills the

> Stop giving in to everyone's de-mands; for, if you don't stop doing this, your life will always remain unbalanced.

ability to utilize the expertise and strengths of oth-ers in order to accomplish tasks.

Some people are trying to start-up business-es and their biggest obstacle is finding suitable help. The sad part is this: a person, for example, may be in need of someone to help them with the accounting, but they are overlooking or have forgotten that they already have a brother who's an accountant, or a cous-in that's a lawyer, a sister who's an interior decorator, or an uncle who has the expertise they need in order to get things going. Most times we already have all of the resources we need in the people around us, but we because we won't open our mouths we suffer needlessly. This is why Satan is able to prevent many people from succeeding in life: God placed around them the resources they need to succeed, but Satan caused rifts in their relationships in order to prevent them from communicating with one another. If you forgive, tear down walls of pride, admit your wrongs and restore the relationships, you will have valuable resources right at your disposal to do what you need to do. Don't fall for Satan's schemes. Whenever necessary, seek help from those around you; but most importantly, seek help from God—His guidance and assistance is invaluable (James 4:1-3).

Take breaks. Take breaks periodically while working on projects. Don't burn yourself out. Let your body and mind rejuvenate. Short fifteen minute breaks at work helps you to recover so that you can tackle any task with fresh energy. Take a break and do things that relax your mind and body. For example, go to a spa, a movie, etc. Vacationing is critically important. If you don't relax your body, you'll get burned out.

Exercise. It's important that you get stress off of you through physical exercise. Stressful work will place a lot of stress on you, and stress is what's known as "a silent killer" because it creeps up on you without you knowing it and brings serious illnesses your way. You have to exercise to survive in situations where you're being pulled in multiple directions. You'll feel better.

CHAPTER 7
STAND TALL
ON THE WATER

$\mathcal{S}$OME PROBLEMS ARE UNAVOIDABLE—THEY'RE simply part of the territory called success. You will never be cool enough, nice enough, or spiritual enough to avoid one problem in particular: jealousy. If you are succeeding in life—your business is picking up, your plans are coming to fruition, you're now climbing that corporate ladder and have inched just that much closer to your career goals, your church's attendance has drastically increased, your family has grown, your marriage has improved, your quality of life has improved, etc.—then there will undoubtedly arise jealous stares and critical words.

A Law of Focus principle is this: Chase after your dreams, not people. People come and go; they help sometimes for a season, and then their season is up; they sway back and forth in their emotions and devotions; the dream, however, remains the same no matter who comes and goes. You don't want to run a business while focusing on people; you want to run a business while focusing on results; and if gaining results mean letting some people go or bring certain people around, then that is what you have to do. Get out of your feelings and get that money.

In business, customer service is the key. People remember less what you say and more how you make them feel. Give people a good experience and they'll patronize your business. Your goal should

> **Chase after your dreams, not people.**

be to create an environment that attracts people, and to create an experience that motivates people to return. After all, if people are not coming back to your business, then your financial dream and security are in jeopardy. So, value people because they are the ones who make or break your business, but don't let your fondness of personalities distract you from focusing on the overall goals and objectives of your business. Don't let family attachments interfere with your productivity, neither allow friendships to interfere with the objectives, quotas, and overall goals of the business or company. Keep everyone on your team, your staff, focused on the objectives and the goals, not on each other. The goal of business is to make money, plain and simple. If you're not making money, you're just doing a hobby or a charity. Also, the purpose of making money is to gain the means to finance the type of life you want to live: provide a better life for your family; finance other dreams and goals; to help those

> **The goal of business is to make money, plain and simple. If you're not making money, you're just doing a hobby or a charity.**

who you want and need to help; etc. The Bible tells us in Ecclesiastes 10:19,

> "Men prepare a meal for enjoyment, and wine makes life merry, and **money is the answer to**

everything." (NASB)

What this is saying is money provides the means for all of the things we want to do in life. Let's be wise and not foolish. Money isn't evil; the love of money is evil; however, money is the tool needed to create a life of fulfillment. You can't even operate in ministry without money. Try keeping the bills paid, or church note paid, or the insurance paid without money. Try engaging in outreach activities such as helping those in need, feeding and clothing those in need, offering programs and classes, etc. without money. Just think about it: On of the first things that happened in the church after the Holy Spirit possessed Believers on the day of Pentecost is worshipers began laying their offerings at the apostles' feet, and the apostles began using the money to meet the needs of the people as revealed in Acts 4:35. God may be trying to redirect you to a different strategy in your ministry that will bring the finances you need. Quit listening to people and start listening to God. Focus on obeying His instructions and He'll send the right people, and the right people will bring increase financially as well as in the other areas (1 Corinthians 3:6-7; Psalm 75:6). And this principle doesn't just apply to ministry, but to other business ventures also.

In the Bible, King Saul messed up because of one thing: he focused less on what God wanted and more on what the people wanted. The Bible says in 1 Samuel 15:11 that God regretted promoting Saul to the position of king because Saul was more of a people-pleaser than he was a God-chaser. Saul lived for the approval and praises of people; and therefore, he lost the favor and approval of God. Placing focus on the people rather than God and His instructions cost Saul everything, as it will you if you operate the same way. Don't throw everything away.

If your focus is on people, personalities, and personal feelings and emotions, then you'll only end up crippling your chances of achieving the things in life that you want and need to achieve. Look at the bigger picture! If a consultant tells you to change the way that you do things for the sake of increasing the sales and customer-ship in your business, then forget about your personal feelings and focus on the things that need to be done to increase business. Don't turn your business into your personal playground used to placate to your fantasies; you'll lose money, and will hence jeopardize your ability to actually live out the desires of your heart. If God is leading you to use a certain gift or talent in order to change your financial situation (I'm not talking about doing anything illegal, unethical and immoral, like stripping, selling drugs, or promoting sinful practices), then drop your pride, get out of your idealistic fantasy world and do what God is telling you to do. Remember: One door will open up other doors; one opportunity will lead to other opportunities; one gift or talent will put you in a position to explore your other dreams. You have a goal, but the path God may be taking you to get to that goal isn't what you anticipated. Just follow God and let Him lead you the way He wants to. Walk by faith, not by sight. God knows what He's doing. He knows what it takes to get you to where you need to be more than you think.

> ...get out of your idealistic fantasy world and do what God is telling you to do.

Today, Bill Gates, the founder of Microsoft, travels the world raising awareness about global epidemics such as disease and starvation; he advocates for solutions to many social crises in our world; but Bill Gates would never be in the position to do what he does today if he didn't first focus on business and making money. It's important to dream, but at some point you must open your eyes and strategize so that you can bring those dreams closer to reality, and the strategizing phase may cause for you to do what you don't want to do. Do what must be done so that you can get into the position where, like Bill Gates, you can do what you want to do. So, take your eyes off of yourself and your friends and family and . . . focus on the goal and the steps to accomplishing it.

DIRTY WORDS

As mentioned earlier, Jesus explained that persecution follows success; so there is nothing that you can do about negative criticism from people who cringe at the fact that you're succeeding in life. You cannot bypass

> It's important to dream, but at some point you must open your eyes and strategize so that you can bring those dreams closer to reality...

criticism, jealousy, envy . . . and hurtful words. The only thing you can do is accept that their shots at you are just a part of the territory. But don't worry about their criticism. Stay focused on your business, on your goals. The Bible says in Ecclesiastes 7:21,

"Do not pay attention to every word people say, or you may hear your servant cursing

you." (NIV)

Powerful!! If you eavesdrop on everyone's conversation, you're bound to hear negative statements about you. That's your fault, though. You should not have been so focused on people's opinions to begin with, worried about what "they" have to say. You subjected your ears to that torture and your spirit to that type of beating. Keep your spirit clean and your mind on that which matters—and everyone else's insults and opinions of you don't matter. So, quit checking your Facebook page to see what they think about you. Do not focus on everyone's opinions in the discussion section under your Youtube clip(s). Take constructive criticism only from your mentors and advisors: those people who know how to lead you to success and pinpoint the areas in your business or career that need improvement. But don't worry about envious, jealous complainers. Just know that complainers aren't going anywhere. Some people are only good at complaining about things— what others have; what they don't have. Individuals such as these have an entitlement mentality and will never put in the work to fulfill their own purposes in life because they have been tricked by Satan into spending all of their time looking at others rather at God. That's their doing. You have no reason to apologize for doing what God told you to do and reaping the benefits of an obedient life. God said in Romans chapter 11 that He would bless those who're obedient to Him just to make unbelievers jealous. So, let God give *the* haters something to talk about!

Peter was walking on water as long as he kept his eyes on Jesus. The second he took his eyes off of Christ, he began to sink. When we take our eyes off of God and His purpose for our lives and start looking at everyone else to see if they like us, agree with what God is doing in and through us, and support us, we end up sink-ing in the waters of fear, suffocating in a sea of opinions, drowning in a sea of comparisons and identity confusion; we

> You have no reason to apologize for doing what God told you to do and reaping the benefits of a obedient life.

lose sight of who God made us and what God cre-ated us for. This will only lead to ruin and defeat in your life. The blessing is if you're currently sinking, you can call out to Jesus to save you, and like He did to Peter, He'll pull you out of the water and give you the supernatural ability to walk on the waters of public opinion, the very waters that drown most individuals who aspire to be great.

THEY'RE WATCHING YOU

God will give you influence with men, which is what you need in order to get where He wants you to be. This is one of the benefits of walking in humility. If a person is arrogant, God won't exalt them. Don't be arrogant (holding a high opinion of yourself). Wait on God. Trust Him. Depend on Him. Do things the right way, His way, and don't cut corners just to get ahead. Don't allow strife to fill your heart and cause you to scheme for power and control. God will give it to you if you're in His will and His timing. There's a season with your name on it. But in the meantime, know that people are watching you. You might not even be in that place of destiny yet, but people can already see the hand of God on your life. It may even surprise you to discover that people who have what you want are already intimidated by you—and you haven't even "arrived" yet. There are people who are following you secretly despite the fact that they have more influence than you. They may have thousands of Facebook followers and you only have hundreds, but they're frightened by you and are copying everything you do and presenting your ideas as their own. Don't be worried about that. Get prepared for people to come around and pull on that which is on the inside of you in secret. No, they'll never give you the credit for their successes, but just know that your humility is going to pay-off. Joseph helped several men while locked-up in that dingy prison dungeon in Egypt, and after those men made it out, they forgot all about him, but God didn't forget about him; God caused a situation to arise that caused Joseph's gift to come to the forefront and him to be recognized. God did it! People who you think will elevate you may not; actually, they may steal your ideas and boot you off to the side because you're unknown; but God is the one who holds the keys to elevation (Job chapter 12). Don't be bitter; be wise. Learn to keep your mouth closed and not tell everything you hear God speaking into your spirit. And if someone does steal your idea, just know that they didn't steal your mind. There's more where that idea came from! One idea doesn't make you. God has multi-

> People who you think will elevate you may not; actually, they may steal your ideas and boot you off to the side because you're unknown; but God is the one who holds the keys to elevation....

ple gifts, ideas, and talents which He has given you. Don't be a one-dimensional person; be multi-faceted as God intended for you to be.

The world has enough imitators as it is. Some might imitate your style, but they can't imitate your creativity. Stay focused and don't get upset over the fact that some people will always like your ideas but never like you. If God likes you, elevation is coming and influence will position you above your haters.

Influence is coming. Elevation is coming. Be who God called you to be. Bloom where God placed you. Stay in your lane. Stay humble before God and focused only on that which He called you to do. You will succeed and be fed in the very presence of your enemies.

> Some might imitate your style, but they can't imitate your creativity.

CHAPTER 8
SPEAK YOUR PLANS

UST ABOUT EVERY SUCCESSFUL PERSON ON THE planet has put into practice this last Law of Focus principle which I'm about to share with you. We see books containing this secret in print topping the best sellers lists all over the globe. This step produces extraordinary results. I'm talking about the power of speaking your destiny. There is power in words.

WHAT ARE WORDS?

Words are more than expressed thoughts. Words are a creative force that God has given you to be and do like Him. God spoke and said, "Let there be . . ." and there was. The only time God made something with His hands is when He made man. All other creation was the result of God's words:

> "By faith we understand that the entire universe was formed at **God's command,** that what we now see did not come from anything that can be seen." (Hebrews 11:3, NLT)

> **"The Word gave life to everything that was created,** and his life brought light to everyone." (John 1:4, NLT)

You and I have the same ability to speak into existence what we want to see done in our lives because our words are "electromagnetic life-forces that can be measured" according to renown

> **Words are a creative force that God has given you to be and do like Him.**

cognitive neuroscientist, Dr. Caroline Leaf. Leaf is a leading researcher in brain science, having a Ph.D.

in Communication Pathology specializing in Neuropsychology. As Leaf basically reveals, words are a substance. If our words can be measured, then they're actually physical in nature. That is amazing! This revelation alone should shift your understanding of the power of words. But there's more! According to other scientific research, we can either make our bodies sick or well just by the power of our thoughts and words in what's known as The Placebo Effect— this is where a person will be given a fake treatment, but because they think it's real, they'll exhibit the effects of being healed. For example, if a person is suffering from a headache and you give them a sugar pill but claim the pill you're giving them is an Aspirin, that person, upon taking the pill after convincing themselves that it's really an Aspirin will actually experience their headache going away. Why? It's not because of the pill, but because they

> ...words are "electro magnetic life-forces that can be measured" according to Dr. Caroline Leaf.

"believe" the pill was real and is curing them of their headache. Without realizing it, they're being healed by their own thoughts. Numerous scientific studies have confirmed this to be a real phenomenon.

Another scientific experiment conducted by a group of Russian scientists discovered something that is even more fascinating than anything else that I've read. In a recent article entitled *Scientists Discover That DNA Can Be Reprogrammed With Words and Frequencies*, it's been discovered that our words are actual frequencies (waves) can alter our genetic codes. That means our words can physically transform our bodies, not just our perceptions.

There was an experiment done by a Japanese researcher named Masaru Emoto where he put rice in three different jars, filled them with water, labeled each jar "Thank you", "You're an idiot" and "Ignored" and then spoke to each jar of rice every day for a month. He'd speak to the jar filled with rice labeled "Thank you" and say "Thank you" to it, and then speak to the jar labeled "You're an idiot" and say "You're an idiot" to it, and then walk right pass the jar labeled "Ignored" without speaking a word to it. At the end of the month, Dr. Emoto gained some amazing results: the jar that he said "Thank you" to each morning, the rice inside began to ferment and let off a sweet fragrance, but the jar

> ...words can physically transform our bodies, not just our perceptions.

he said "You're an idiot" to, the rice inside it began to rot; the jar that Dr. Emoto completely ignored altogether had a very interesting outcome: it was more rotted than the jar labeled "You're an idiot"—

Dr. Masaru Emoto's Rice & Water Experiment

"Thank You"   **"You're An Idiot"**   *Ignored*

Dr. Emoto's conclusion was that words can transform the molecular structure of DNA, and in this case, it changed the molecular structure of the rice in all three of the jars. Regarding the ignored and neglected jar, it was concluded that by not speaking to the rice within it, the effects of neglect were more damaging than bad words. So, not speaking to someone is more damaging than speaking to them in a negative manner. By ignoring a person, the same effect that not touching a baby or child has as revealed by science (not touching a baby can actually lead to that baby's death) can similarly occur. Basically, the worst abuse is neglect. Even if someone shows you negative attention, that is still better than being totally ignored as if you are not even there.

Whoa! This might explain why some women will stay with abusive men: they desperately crave attention, even if it is negative attention. Their biggest fear is being alone and ignored.

Other people have repeated Dr. Emoto's rice experiment. Some experienced similar results as that of Dr. Emoto's; some didn't. But when we combine all of the newest and latest research that has emerged as a result of scientific study in the area of words, it's clear that thoughts and words can physically transform our bodies, even if only in microscopic ways we can't see with our natural eyes—changes that would require specialized scientific tools to measure. There is also one thing that all of this research validates: it proves what the Bible says about words.

> "The Spirit alone gives eternal life. Human effort accomplishes nothing. **And the very words I have spoken to you are spirit and life.**" (John 6:63, NLT)

> "Kind words are like honey--sweet to the soul and **healthy for the body.**" (Proverbs 16:24, NLT)

"Death and life are in the power of the tongue, And those who love it will eat its fruit." (Proverbs 18:24, NASB)

So, according to the Bible, words are "spirit and life" (meaning an actual substance), they can either heal or sicken our physical bodies, and they can bring life or death our way. That's a lot of power!!!

WHAT WORLD ARE YOU CREATING FOR YOURSELF?

Every day of your life you are shaping your world—you are either speaking life or death over yourself, or you are speaking healing or sickness over your body. Every day of your life you are speaking faith or doubt into your spirit, and you're reaping the fruit of those words. As a Christian, it does no good to speak fear and doubt and expect God to bless me. God made it explicitly clear that our words can either cause blessings or curses to arise in our lives (Hebrews 3:7-4:2; James 1:6-7; Matthew 21:21). God won't even move in our situations if we believe the wrong words: the ones filled with doubt and disbelief. It's better to go ahead and believe God for a miracle than to doubt Him and remain in the state that you are. Worrying isn't going to improve anything—actually, worry will only make things worse.

Speak life into your situation. Declare God's promises over your life daily. God instructs us in Isaiah 43:26 to put Him in remembrance of His Word. Not that God forgot. But when we speak His Word, we authorize Him to move on our behalves. Isaiah 55:11 tells us God's Word will never return to Him void, but it will accomplish what it set out to do. In Jeremiah 1:12, God said He watches over His Word to perform it. And in Psalm 103:20, God revealed to us that His angels excel in strength to perform His Word whenever we speak and declare it. This is why as a child of God your words matter so much: they are either authorizing God or the devil to operate in your life.

When a person is spiritually ignorant, they will authorize demons to operate in their lives without realizing it. They will speak curses and then end up experiencing them. In many cases, people who're into the occult take this spiritual Law of Focus and use it in the wrong way: they authorize demon spirits

> This is why as a child of God your words matter so much: they are either authorizing God or the devil to operate in your life.

disguised as "spirit guides" to operate in their lives and bring blessings their way, not knowing that they are giving Satan power over them. Many people will testify that those spirit guides always appear friendly in the beginning, but they reveal their true identities at some later point. God's Word forbids that we talk to spirits, ghosts, try to contact the dead, and engage in other similar practices in Deuteronomy 18:9-12, which says,

> "When you enter the land the LORD your God is giving you, be very careful not to imitate the detestable customs of the nations living there. For example, never sacrifice your son or daughter as a burnt offering. And do not let your people practice fortune-telling, or use sorcery, or interpret omens, or engage in witchcraft, or cast spells, or function as mediums or psychics, or call forth the spirits of the dead. Anyone who does these things is detestable to the LORD. It is because the other nations have done these detestable things that the LORD your God will drive them out ahead of you."

Demons do disguise themselves as the spirits of the deceased (our dead loved ones or people from earth's past); hence, they are called "familiar spirits" in the Bible (*familiar* meaning they disguise themselves as that which we're familiar with). Also, demons will bring blessings our way, but at a serious cost: our souls. What a foolish decision to sell your soul just for temporary material possessions.

God desires to be the source of the blessings in our lives. And yes, God's blessings come with a requirement as well: We must be willing to obey and glorify Him and Him alone. When we obey God, it then becomes our right, duty, and privilege to speak what we want to see done, provided that our requests aren't sinful, of course. That's the right 1 John 5:1-15 tells us we have. EXERCISE IT!!!

Philippians 4:6 tells us,

"Be anxious for nothing, but in everything by prayer and supplication with thanksgiving let your requests be made known to God." (NASB)

The word "supplications" in the Greek is defined as "a specific request." So, as a child of God, you are to be detailed and specific in what you want and speak it in prayer. How many clients do you want over the next 6 months specifically? Exactly how much money are you looking to make through your business in a single year? Give God your quotas, your objectives in other words. Be specific. How do you want your future husband/wife to look? How many kids do you want exactly? Do you want boys? Girls? And if so, how many boys and/or girls? What kind of car do you want to drive? How do you want your house to look? Where do you want to live? Etc. That's how you talk to God—you share with Him every detail of your dream(s).

> The word "supplications" in the Greek is defined as "a specific request." So, as a child of God, you are to be detailed and specific in what you want and speak it in prayer.

DECLARE YOUR INTENTIONS

Investment banker, Michael Kendrick, in his book, *Rich Forever*, describes the process he underwent to arrive at a level of extraordinary success in his career. He stated that, as a skeptic, he was skeptical of what many people call The Law of Attraction. Being that he was a Christian and was already aware of the dangers of gravitating towards the occult techniques taught in the many books that teach that concept, he vowed to avoid them all together; however, God began to impress upon his heart to implement many of the concepts found in those books with the true understanding of their purpose and usage. Kendrick later discovered that these concepts aren't some *secret* passed down by men and women that tapped into a hidden knowledge, but these concepts were originally derived from the Bible. God revealed to us that *as a man thinketh, so is he* in His Word. God told us that "the fear of the wicked shall come upon him, but the righteous will stand as bold as a lion" in Proverbs 10:24. That's the Law of Attraction in a nutshell. Your spirit will attract your reality; and your spirit is affected by the words you both speak and entertain (Luke 6:45). So, if you want to attract the right future, fill your heart and mind with God's Word. Meditate on God's Word day and night and then you'll see the fruit of it in your life.

> Your spirit will attract your reality; and your spirit is affected by the very words you speak and entertain....

Kendrick took what he learned from those other writings and came up with an interesting way to view what happens when we speak what we want to see happen in our lives—a practice that he credits as being the number one tool that brought success into his life despite his many degrees and training. What he discovered is when we speak out loud the things we want to see happen in our lives, our subconscious minds actually get busy working to make our stated requests a reality. He called this The Law of Intentionality. He used the example of desiring a certain type of car. He declared his intention to purchase a red Jeep, and after speaking his desire, his subconscious mind began to notice red Jeeps everywhere he went. Before stating his intention, red Jeeps were all around him, but he had never really noticed them before—his subconscious mind never picked-up on their presences.

According to this principle, when you openly state out loud what you intend to see and/or do, your subconscious mind will begin working to make you more aware of these things. You change the trajectory of your life through your stated intentions. State your intentions. Verbally speak what you want to see, do, accomplish, gain, receive, and experience in your life. SPEAK GOD'S PROMISES MADE TO YOU OUT LOUD EVERYDAY! And when you speak these things, make sure to record them on a recording device: a cellphone, ipad, tape recorder, etc. Why? Because you'll need to go back and listen to your words periodically in order to keep yourself reminded and focused and to also have a reference point to refer back to at later points in your life. As Mr. Kendrick experienced, in his latter years, while experiencing success beyond his wildest dreams, one day while cleaning out his house he stumbled upon some of his recordings which he made when starting his journey towards success, and he was freaked out by what he heard: everything that he declared his future to be was exactly what he was now experiencing—from way his house would look to the type of car he would be driving and much more.

Write the vision God gave you and make it plain (easy to understand and picture in your mind) and then speak it daily, and then you will experience, as did Mr. Kendrick, that the things you declare over your life will eventually become your reality.

Now grab a pen and a piece of paper and get busy writing out your vision for your life and speaking your future into existence. What are you waiting for? LET'S GO!

ALSO AVAILABLE

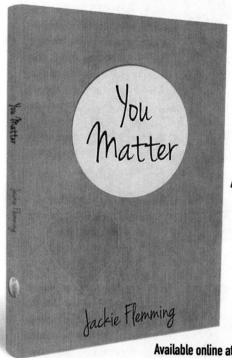

You
Matter

Jackie Flemming

In Jackie Flemming's book "You Matter" you will discover just how important you are to God. This beautifully written and stylishly designed book will open your eyes to your significance and importance like never before. Discover your value and what God has given you to make a difference in this world.

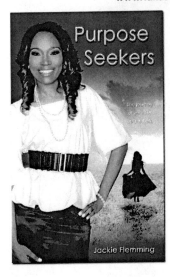
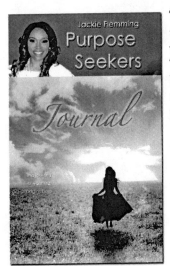

OTHER BOOKS BY T&J PUBLISHERS
www.TandJPublishers.com

In this book by Timothy Flemming, Jr. you will learn from the life of David how to walk in extreme faith. You will discover how to face and conquer every intenal obstacle standing in your way and become the bold, daring, courageous giant killer God called you to be.

Available on Amazon and
Barnes&Noble.com
$16.95 174 pgs.

This book by Timothy Flemming, Jr. contains startling revelations concerning end-times events. It covers the rise and nature of the antichrist, the identities of the counterfeit messiahs Jesus prophesied would come, the rise of occultism in society, the creation of the New World Order, and more.

Available on Amazon.com
and
Barnes&Noble.com
$21.95 500 pgs.

ABOUT THE AUTHOR

Jackie Flemming as an entrepreneur, model, actress, author, motivational speaker, minister. She is married to Timothy Flemming, Jr., and has three children: Timothy 3rd, Timera, and Jeremiah Flemming.

Her professional career includes modeling for Liz Claiborne, Chicos, and other several promotions. She is the founder of Unique Ladies Boutique, which focuses on women's apparel.

As an entrepreneur, Jackie left corporate America in 2014 and stepped into business for herself as an author, motivational speaker, and success coach. She started The Model In You (an empowerment program for girls) and the Purpose Seekers Network. She combines the uniqueness, fun, and glamor from her modeling background with her passion for helping others to lift their self-image and confidence, which she has cultivated over the years while working with individuals from all walks of life—from group homes to women's ministries—to transform and impact lives.

Jackie is the author of *Purpose Seekers*, *Purpose Seekers Journal*, *You Matter*, and *Stay Focused*.

For more information, go to: www.LadyJackie.com

CPSIA information can be obtained at www.ICGtesting.com
Printed in the USA
LVOW10s1434080216

474185LV00001B/2/P

9 780996 216593